Looking at Clouds

Susan Ring

When you go outside and look up at the sky, you will probably see clouds. Look again and they will have changed.

Where do clouds come from? Why are they always changing?

How a Cloud Forms and Changes

Millions of these droplets join together and form clouds.

When warm air rises in the sky, it contains very tiny droplets of water.

Wind can also push two clouds together to form a bigger cloud.

Wind can make some clouds drift away.

Clouds come in all different shapes and sizes. They can be pretty to look at, but did you know that they also give us messages? *105*

Scientists who study the weather are called **meteorologists** (mee-tee-uh-ROL-uh-jists). They watch the winds and the clouds. They use what they see to help predict the weather.

Meteorologists track hurricanes by watching clouds. They take pictures from satellites in space.

Of course, not all clouds mean that a hurricane is on the way. Different kinds of clouds mean different kinds of weather.

This satellite picture shows huge hurricane clouds spinning and swirling around.

8

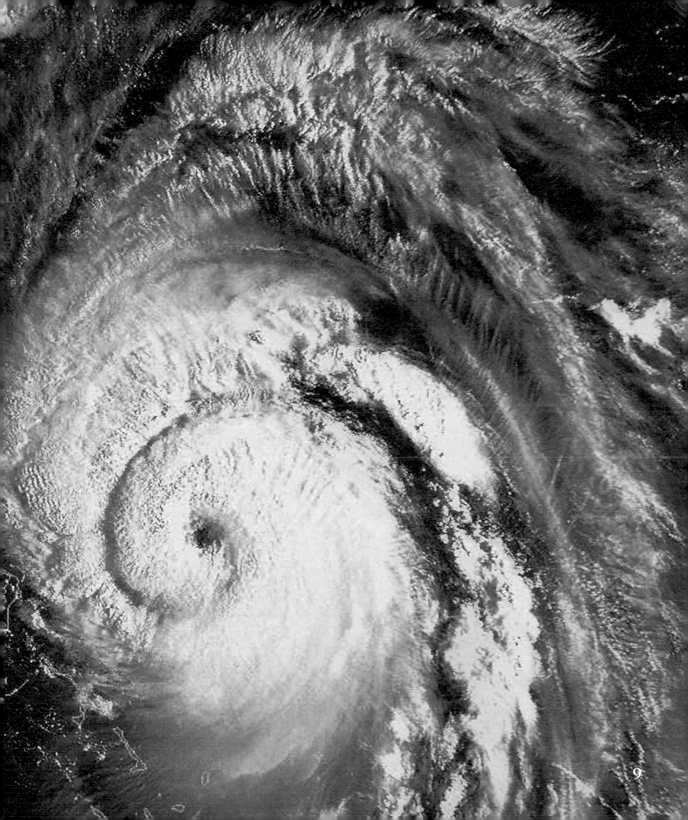

These big, white fluffy clouds are called **cumulus** (KUME-yoo-luss) clouds. They look like huge heaps of cotton when the sky is blue.

Airplane pilots watch the clouds. They like seeing cumulus clouds like these. Cumulus clouds tell them that the weather should be fine for flying.

When cumulus clouds get very full with water, they get bigger and darker. They become **nimbus** (NIM-buss) clouds.

Farmers watch the clouds. They need to know the best time to plant, water, and harvest their crops. When they see nimbus clouds, they prepare for heavy rain or snow.

Stratus (STRA-tuss) clouds are like huge grey blankets covering the sky. Usually you just see the lowest layer of these clouds. When it is cold, they might bring a light snowfall. When it is warmer, stratus clouds sometimes bring tiny raindrops called drizzle.

14

High **cirrus** (SEER-uss) clouds look like wispy curls or a horse's tail. Cirrus clouds usually bring rain or snow within 24 hours.

15

So, the next time you look at clouds, think about what you see. Are they fluffy like cotton? Are they high and wispy like a horse's tail? Are they a dark blanket across the sky? What messages do you see in the clouds?